Program Authors

Peter Afflerbach

Camille Blachowicz

Candy Dawson Boyd

Elena Izquierdo

Connie Juel

Edward Kame'enui

Donald Leu

Jeanne Paratore

Sam Sebesta

Deborah Simmons

Alfred Tatum

Sharon Vaughn

Susan Watts Taffe

Karen Kring Wixson

D1377714

Glenview, Illinois • Boston, Massachusetts • Chandler, Arizona • Upper Saddle River, New Jersey

We dedicate Reading Street to
Peter Jovanovich.

His wisdom, courage,
and passion for education
are an inspiration to us all.

About the Cover Artist
Rob Hefferan likes to reminisce about the simple life he had as a child growing up in Cheshire, when his biggest worry was whether to have fish fingers or Alphabetti Spaghetti for tea. The faces, colors, and shapes from that time are a present-day inspiration for his artwork.

ISBN-13: 978-0-328-47850-7
ISBN-10:   0-328-47850-4
1 2 3 4 5 6 7 8 9 10 V011 13 12 11 10 09

Dear Texas Reader,

Now that you know about traveling down Reading Street, how would you like to meet George Washington? Do you know who George Washington is? If not, you'll soon find out. You're in for a treat.

George Washington, Little Panda, and other characters are all waiting to meet you.

As always, you'll need to bring along all your special skills for reading, writing, and thinking.

Buckle up, and let's get started.

Sincerely,
The Authors

Changes All Around Us

 How do changes affect us?

Big Book

4

Week 2

Unit 3 Contents

Week 3

Historical Fiction • Social Studies
George Washington Visits by Dennis Fertig

Big Book

Week 4

Animal Fantasy • Science
Farfallina and Marcel by Holly Keller

Trade Book

Week 5

Week 6

Don Leu
The Internet Guy

Right before our eyes, the nature of reading and learning is changing. The Internet and other technologies create new opportunities, new solutions, and new literacies. New reading comprehension skills are required online. They are increasingly important to our students and our society.

Those of us on the Reading Street team are here to help you on this new, and very exciting, journey.

See It!

- Big Question Video

- Concept Talk Video

- Envision It! Animations

- eReaders

Hear It!

- Amazing Words *Sing With Me*

- eSelections

- Grammar Jammer

Adam and Kim **play at the beach.**

Concept Talk Video

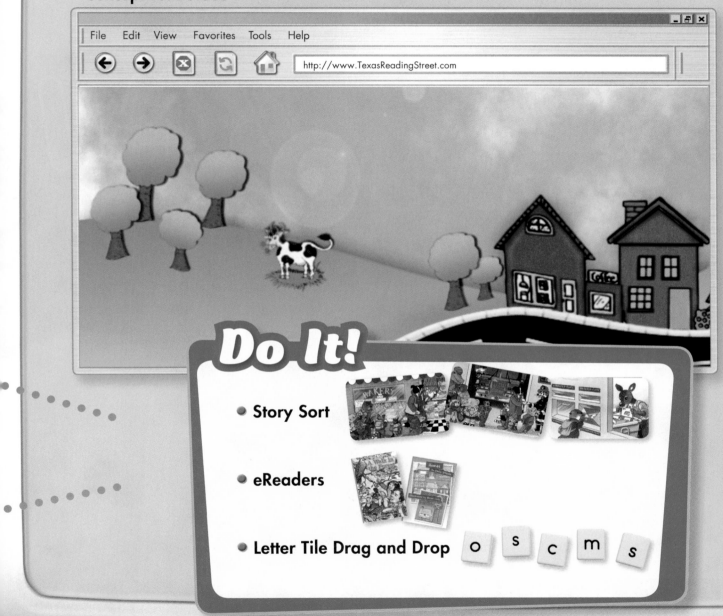

File   Edit   View   Favorites   Tools   Help

http://www.TexasReadingStreet.com

Do It!

- **Story Sort**

- **eReaders**

- **Letter Tile Drag and Drop**   o s c m s

Changes All Around Us

THE BIG
?

How do changes
affect us?

TEKS

K.2.E.1 Recognize spoken alliteration or groups of words that begin with the same spoken onset or initial sound. **K.2.H.1** Isolate the initial sound in spoken one-syllable words.

Let's Listen for

Read Together

Initial Sounds

● Point to a nest. Say the word. Say the beginning sound.

■ Point to the baby. Say the word. Say the beginning sound.

▲ Find three pictures that begin with /n/. With /b/.

★ Point to these pictures and say the words: *nest, neighbor, fence.* Do they begin the same? What about *bird, baby, bottle?*

♥ Name other words that begin with /n/. With /b/.

READING STREET ONLINE
BIG QUESTION VIDEO
www.TexasReadingStreet.com

12

Comprehension

Envision It!

Compare and Contrast

**READING STREET ONLINE
PICTURE IT! ANIMATION**
www.TexasReadingStreet.com

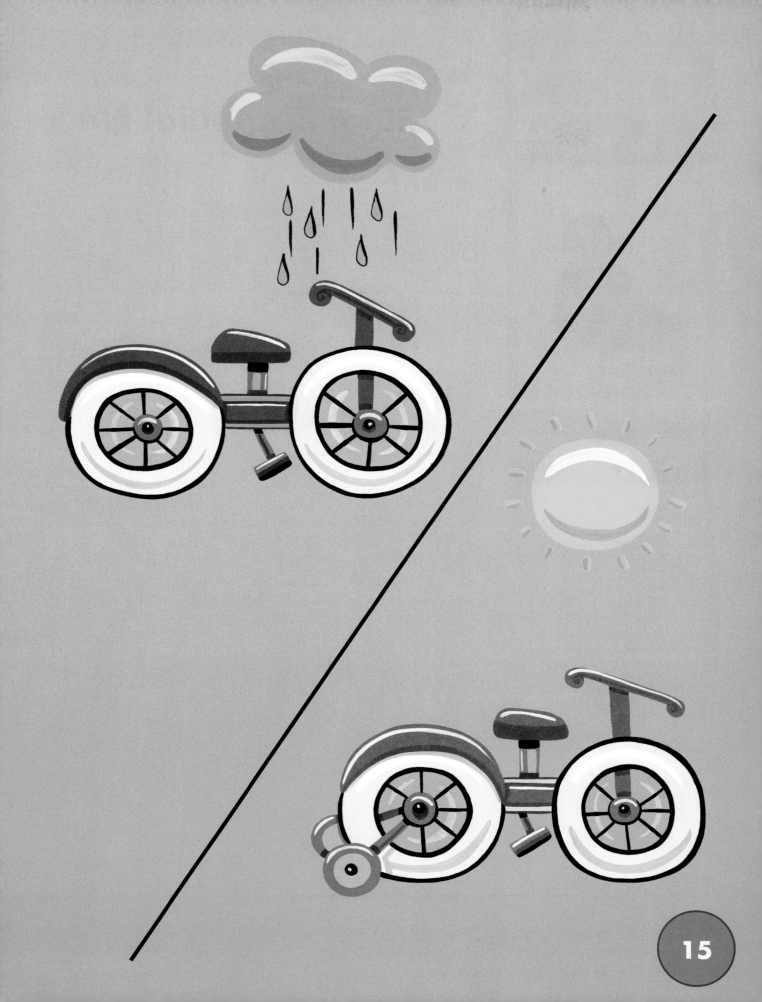

Envision It! | Sounds to Know

Bb

baby

READING STREET ONLINE
ALPHABET CARDS
www.TexasReadingStreet.com

Phonics

Initial *Bb*, Initial *Nn*

Words I Can Blend

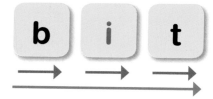

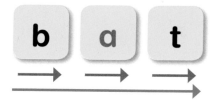

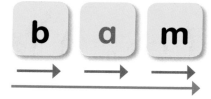

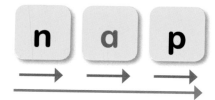

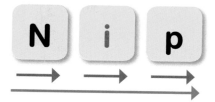

Words I Can Read

me

with

she

Sentences I Can Read

1. Nip is with me.

2. She is my cat.

3. Is Nip with Nat?

TEKS
K.3.A.1 Identify the common sounds that letters represent. K.3.B.1 Use knowledge of letter-sound relationships to decode regular words in text. K.3.D Identify and read at least 25 high-frequency words from a commonly used list.

Phonics

I Can Read!

Decodable Reader

- ● Consonant *Bb*
  bat

- ■ Consonant *Nn*
  can
  Nat
  Nan

- ▲ High-Frequency Words
  she
  with
  me

- ★ Read the story.

READING STREET ONLINE
DECODABLE eBOOKS
www.TexasReadingStreet.com

Decodable Reader 13

Nat!

Written by Patricia Crotty
Illustrated by Dan Vick

Can Nat bat it?
Nat can bat it.

Can Nat tap it?
Nat can tap it.

Can Nat pat it?
Nat can pat it.

Nan can bat it.
She can bat.

Can Nat sip it?
Nat can sip it.

Nat sat with me.

Nat can bat!

TEKS

K.10.B.1 Retell important events in a text, heard or read. ★Tell how facts, ideas, characters, settings, or events are the same and/or different.

Big Book

Envision It! | Retell

1

2

3

4

5

6

READING STREET ONLINE
RETELL
www.TexasReadingStreet.com

26

Think, Talk, and Write

Read Together

1. How does a baby panda change as it grows? Text to World

2. How are a baby panda and an adult panda alike? How are they different?

Compare and Contrast

3. Look back and write.

27

TEKS

K.5.C Identify and sort pictures of objects into conceptual categories. **K.22** Share information and ideas by speaking audibly and clearly using the conventions of language.

Let's  It!

Vocabulary

- What do you see that is black?
- What do you see that is green?
- What do you see that is brown?

Listening and Speaking

- Act like a character from the story.
- Act like your favorite character from a story.

Vocabulary

Color Words

black

green

brown

Respond to Literature
Drama

Be a good speaker!

TEKS

K.7.A Respond to rhythm and rhyme in poetry through identifying a regular beat and similarities in word sounds. **RC-K.B.2** Respond to questions about text. **RC-K.F** Make connections to ideas in other texts and discuss textual evidence.

Let's Practice It!

Poems

● Listen to the two poems.

■ Recite each poem. Sway in time to its rhythm.

▲ Which words rhyme in the first poem? in the second poem?

★ How are the two poems alike?

♥ In the second poem, what does the poet say a star is like?

Star Light, Star Bright

Twinkle, Twinkle, LIttle Star

TEKS

K.2.E.1 Recognize spoken alliteration or groups of words that begin with the same spoken onset or initial sound. **K.2.H.1** Isolate the initial sound in spoken one-syllable words.

Phonemic Awareness

Let's Listen for

Initial Sounds

Read Together

● Point to the red cap. Say *red*. Say the beginning sound.

■ Find three pictures that begin with /r/.

▲ Name other words that begin like *red*.

★ Point to these pictures and say the words: *rose*, *red*, *ribbon*. Do they begin the same? What about *nest*, *baby*, *bird*?

READING STREET ONLINE
BIG QUESTION VIDEO
www.TexasReadingStreet.com

TEKS

K.6.A.3 Identify elements of a story including key events.

Comprehension

Envision It!

Literary Elements

**READING STREET ONLINE
PICTURE IT! ANIMATION**
www.TexasReadingStreet.com

Characters

Setting

Plot

TEKS

K.3.B.1 Use letter-sound relationships to decode regular words in text and independent of content. **K.3.D** Identify and read at least 25 high-frequency words from a commonly used list. **Also K.3.C.**

Envision It! | **Sounds to Know**

Rr

river

READING STREET ONLINE
ALPHABET CARDS
www.TexasReadingStreet.com

Phonics

🔄 Initial *Rr*

Words I Can Blend

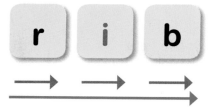

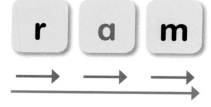

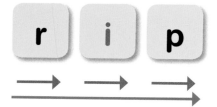

Words I Can Read

me

with

she

Sentences I Can Read

1. Nan ran with me.

2. She ran to my cat.

3. We ran with Ric.

TEKS

K.3.A.1 Identify the common sounds that letters represent. **K.3.B.1** Use knowledge of letter-sound relationships to decode regular words in text. **K.3.D** Identify and read at least 25 high-frequency words from a commonly used list.

Phonics

I Can Read!

Decodable Reader

- Consonant *Rr*
  Rip
  rat
  ran
  Rap

- High-Frequency Words
  the
  a
  she
  with
  me

▲ Read the story.

Decodable Reader 14

Rip with Rap

Written by Peggy Lee
Illustrated by Lucy Smythe

Rip the rat can sit.

Rip sat in a cap.
Rip sat.

Rip ran in the can.
Rip ran.

Rip sat in the can.
Rip sat.

Rip can bat the cap.
She can bat it.

Rip is with me.
Rip can sit.

Rip can nap.
Rap can bat.

TEKS

K.6.A.3 Identify elements of a story including key events. **K.8.A.1** Retell a main event from a story read aloud. **RC-K.E.2** Act out important events in stories. **RC-K.F.1** Make connections to own experiences.

Envision It! Retell

Trade Book

Think, Talk, and Write

1. What new things have you learned to do? **Text to Self**

2.

Beginning	
Middle	
End	

Choose an important part of the story. Act it out with some friends.  Plot

3. Look back and write.

47

TEKS

K.5.A Identify and use words that name actions. K.21.B.1 Follow oral directions that involve a short related sequence of actions. K.22 Share information and ideas by speaking audibly and clearly using the conventions of language.

Let's Learn It!

Vocabulary

- Talk about the pictures.
- Name actions you do.

Listening and Speaking

- Show how to do something.
- Tell how you do it.
- ▲ Speak in complete sentences.

Vocabulary

Action Words

walk

run

fly

swim

Sequence

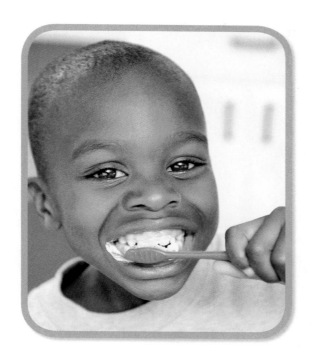

Be a good speaker!

TEKS

K.6.A Identify elements of a story including setting, character, and key events. **K.6.D** Recognize recurring phrases and characters in traditional fairy tales from various cultures. **K.8.B.1** Describe characters in a story.

Rumpelstiltskin

Let's Practice It!

Fairy Tale

● Listen to the fairy tale.

■ What do the words *Once upon a time* tell you about the story?

▲ When and where does the story take place?

★ Describe the character Rumpelstiltskin.

♥ What happens in threes in the story?

51

Phonemic Awareness

Let's Listen for

Initial Sounds

Read Together

● Point to a deer. Say the word. Say the beginning sound.

■ Point to *kick*. Say the word. Say the beginning sound.

▲ Find three pictures that begin with /d/ and /k/.

★ Name other words that begin with /d/ and /k/.

READING STREET ONLINE
BIG QUESTION VIDEO
www.TexasReadingStreet.com

52

Comprehension

Envision It!

Cause and Effect

READING STREET ONLINE
PICTURE IT! ANIMATION
www.TexasReadingStreet.com

TEKS

K.3.A.1 Identify the common sounds that letters represent. **K.3.B** Use letter-sound relationships to decode regular words in text and independent of content. **K.3.C** Recognize that new words are created when letters are changed, added, or deleted.

Envision It! | Sounds to Know

Kk

koala

READING STREET ONLINE
ALPHABET CARDS
www.TexasReadingStreet.com

Phonics

Initial *Kk,* Initial *Dd*

Words I Can Blend

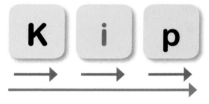

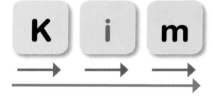

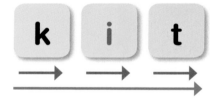

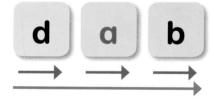

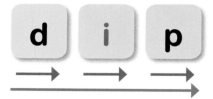

Words I Can Read

see

look

Sentences I Can Read

1. I see Kip.

2. We can look at Kim.

3. Look, can we see Kip?

TEKS
K.3.A.1 Identify the common sounds that letters represent. **K.3.B.1** Use knowledge of letter-sound relationships to decode regular words in text. **K.3.D** Identify and read at least 25 high-frequency words from a commonly used list.

Phonics

I Can Read!

Decodable Reader

● Consonant *Dd*
  did
  Dad
  kid

■ Consonant *Kk*
  kid

▲ High-Frequency Words
  see
  the
  look

★ Read the story.

READING STREET ONLINE
DECODABLE eBOOKS
www.TexasReadingStreet.com

Dad Did

Written by June Harper
Illustrated by Bethany Mills

Decodable Reader 15

Did Dad see the cat?
Dad did.

Did Dad look at it?
Dad did.

Did Dad see the rat?
Dad did.

Did Dad look at it?
Dad did.

Did Dad see the kid?
Dad did.

Did Dad look at it?
Dad did.

Dad can.
Dad did.

TEKS

K.8.A.1 Retell a main event from a story read aloud. **RC-K.F.2** Make connections to ideas in other texts. ★ Identify what happens in a text and why it happens.

Big Book

Envision It! Retell

Think, Talk, and Write

1. How is this town's celebration like the one in *We Are So Proud*? **Text to Text**

2. What did Daniel and Father do in the story? Why did they do it?  **Cause and Effect**

DECEMBER 26, 1776 – JANUARY 2, 1777

3. Look back and write.

TEKS

K.5.A Identify and use words that name positions. **K.2.C.1** Orally generate rhymes in response to spoken words. **K.23.A.2** Follow agreed-upon rules for discussion, including speaking one at a time.

Let's Learn It!

Vocabulary

- ● Talk about the pictures.
- ■ Put your hand over your head.
- ▲ Put your finger under your nose.
- ★ Put your hand on your knee.
- ♥ Sit in a circle around your teacher.

Listening and Speaking

- ● Name words that rhyme with *man*, *black*, and *cat*.
- ■ Say a rhyme.
- ▲ Make up a rhyme of your own.

Vocabulary

Position Words

over

under

on

around

Recite Rhymes

Be a good speaker!

69

TEKS

K.4.B.1 Ask questions about texts read aloud. **K.9.A.1** Identify the topic of an informational text heard. **K.11.A.1** Follow pictorial directions. **RC-K.B.1** Ask questions about text.

Can Celery Sip?

Step 1

Let's Practice It!

Science Experiment

● Listen to the science experiment.

■ What is this experiment about?

▲ In which step do you use the scissors?

★ What makes the celery change color?

♥ What questions do you have about the experiment?

70

Step 2

Step 3

Step 4

Step 5

71

TEKS
K.2.C.1 Orally generate rhymes in response to spoken words.
K.2.E.1 Recognize spoken alliteration or groups of words that begin with the same spoken onset or initial sound. **K.2.H.1** Isolate the initial sound in spoken one-syllable words.

Phonemic Awareness

Let's Listen for

Read Together

Initial Sounds

● Point to the fence. Say the word. Say the beginning sound.

■ Find three things that begin with /f/, like *fence*.

▲ Say these words: *feet, food, dress*. Do they begin with the same sound? What about *first, finger, fast*?

★ What rhymes with *fish*?

READING STREET ONLINE
BIG QUESTION VIDEO
www.TexasReadingStreet.com

72

Comprehension

Envision It!

Literary Elements

READING STREET ONLINE
PICTURE IT! ANIMATION
www.TexasReadingStreet.com

Characters

Setting

Plot

TEKS

K.3.B.1 Use letter-sound relationships to decode regular words in text and independent of content.
K.3.C.3 Recognize that new words are created when letters are deleted.

Envision It! | Sounds to Know

Ff

fountain

Phonics

Initial *Ff*

Words I Can Blend

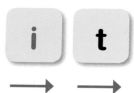

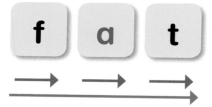

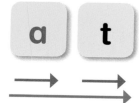

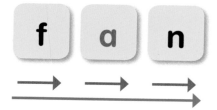

Words I Can Read

see

look

Sentences I Can Read

1. We look for a fin.
2. I see a fin!
3. Look at it.

TEKS

K.3.A.1 Identify the common sounds that letters represent. K.3.B.1 Use knowledge of letter-sound relationships to decode regular words in text. K.3.D Identify and read at least 25 high-frequency words from a commonly used list.

Phonics

I Can Read!

Decodable Reader

● Consonant *Ff*
fan
fat
fit

■ High-Frequency Words
see
a
look
the

▲ Read the story.

READING STREET ONLINE
DECODABLE eBOOKS
www.TexasReadingStreet.com

In the Kit!

Written by Leon Cross
Illustrated by Jeff Blake

Decodable Reader 16

Kip can see a kit.

Kip can look in it.

Kip can see a fan.

Kip can fan.
Fan, Kip, fan.

Kip can see a fat cat.

Kip can pat.
Pat, Kip, pat.

Kip can fit it in the kit.

TEKS

K.6.A.3 Identify elements of a story including key events. **K.8.A.1** Retell a main event from a story read aloud. **RC-K.E.2** Act out important events in stories. **RC-K.F.1** Make connections to own experiences.

Envision It! | Retell

Tradebook

Think, Talk, and Write

1. Which grows like you? Text to Self

2.

Beginning	
Middle	
End	

Choose an important part of the story. Act it out with some friends. Plot

3. Look back and write.

87

TEKS

K.21.A Listen attentively by facing speakers and asking questions to clarify information. **K.22** Share information and ideas by speaking audibly and clearly using the conventions of language.

Let's
Learn
It!

Vocabulary

● Talk about the pictures.

■ Show you are happy.

▲ When might you feel sad?

★ Show you are excited.

♥ When might you be surprised?

Listening and Speaking

● Tell how you've grown.

Vocabulary

Words for Feelings

happy

 sad

excited

 surprised

Oral Presentation

Be a good speaker!

TEKS

K.6.A.3 Identify elements of a story including key events. **K.6.B** Discuss the big idea (theme) of a well-known fable and connect it to personal experience. **K.8.A.1** Retell a main event from a story read aloud. **RC-K.B.2** Respond to questions about text.

Let's Practice It!

Fable

● Listen to the fable.

■ What problem do the mice have?

▲ What is the young mouse's idea?

★ What does the old mouse say about this idea?

♥ How can the fable's moral help you with your ideas?

The Mice and The Cat

91

Phonemic Awareness

Let's Listen for

Read Together

Initial Sounds

● Say *Oscar*. What sound do you hear at the beginning of *Oscar*?

■ Find three pictures that begin with /o/.

▲ Name other words that begin with /o/.

★ Say these words: *Oscar, Otto, oxen*? Do they begin the same? What about *April, olive, onion*?

**READING STREET ONLINE
BIG QUESTION VIDEO**
www.TexasReadingStreet.com

BOOK SALE

92

Comprehension

Envision It!

Draw Conclusions

READING STREET ONLINE
PICTURE IT! ANIMATION
www.TexasReadingStreet.com

Happy Happy Happy

TEKS

K.3.B.1 Use letter-sound relationships to decode regular words in text and independent of content.
K.3.C.3 Recognize that new words are created when letters are deleted.

Envision It! | Sounds to Know

Oo

otter

READING STREET ONLINE
ALPHABET CARDS
www.TexasReadingStreet.com

Phonics

Short o

Words I Can Blend

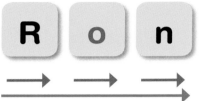

R o n

→ → →

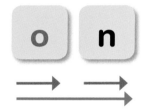

o n

→ →

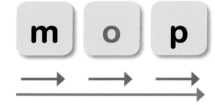

m o p

→ → →

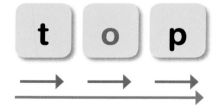

t o p

→ → →

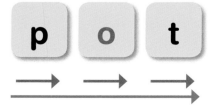

p o t

→ → →

Words I Can Read

they

you

of

Sentences I Can Read

1. Can you see me?
2. They can see me.
3. I am on top of Dad.

TEKS

K.3.A.1 Identify the common sounds that letters represent. K.3.B.1 Use knowledge of letter-sound relationships to decode regular words in text. K.3.D Identify and read at least 25 high-frequency words from a commonly used list.

Phonics

I Can Read!

Decodable Reader

- Short *Oo*
  Tom
  mop
  on
  top
  cot
  Dot

- High-Frequency Words
  of
  the
  they
  look
  you

▲ Read the story.

**READING STREET ONLINE
DECODABLE eBOOKS**
www.TexasReadingStreet.com

The Mop

Written by Donald Newman
Illustrated by Marcia Geller

**Decodable
Reader
17**

Can Tom mop?
Tom can mop.

Tom can nap on
top of the cot.

Can Dot mop?
Dot can mop.

Dot can sit on
top of the cot.

Can Pat mop?
Pat can mop.

Pat can fit on
top of the cot.

They look at the mop.
Can you mop?

TEKS

K.10.B.1 Retell important facts in a text, heard or read. **RC-K.F.3** Make connections to the larger community.

Envision It! | Retell

Then and Now

Written by Tracy Sato
Illustrated by Ute Simon

Big Book

Think, Talk, and Write

1. How have games changed over the years? Text to World

2. How would our lives be different if we still used these things? Draw Conclusions

3. Look back and write.

TEKS

K.22 Share information and ideas by speaking audibly and clearly using the conventions of language. K.23.A.1 Follow agreed-upon rules for discussion, including taking turns.

Let's Learn It!

Vocabulary

● Talk about the pictures.

■ Look around for things that are new and old.

▲ Tell about something that is fast.

★ Tell about something that is slow.

Listening and Speaking

● Leave a message for a friend.

■ Tell whom the message is for and whom it is from.

Vocabulary

Words for Opposites

new

old

fast

slow

Messages and Letters

Be a good speaker!

How Coyote Helped People

1

Let's Practice It!

Folk Tale

● Listen to the folk tale.

■ What two things does the folk tale explain?

▲ What can you learn from the way Coyote behaves?

★ Coyote appears in many Native American folk tales. Why do you think this is so?

TEKS

K.2.E.1 Recognize spoken alliteration or groups of words that begin with the same spoken onset or initial sound. **K.2.H.1** Isolate the initial sound in spoken one-syllable words.

Let's Listen for

Initial Sounds

Read Together

● Say the sound you hear at the beginning of *octopus, bed, nest, red, desk, car, fun.*

■ Point to the *octopus.* Find another picture that begins like *octopus.*

▲ Now find pictures that begin with /b/, /n/, /r/, /d/, /k/, /f/.

★ Say *octopus, otter, ox.* What sound do you hear at the beginning of these words?

READING STREET ONLINE
BIG QUESTION VIDEO
www.TexasReadingStreet.com

112

Comprehension

Envision It!

Main Idea

READING STREET ONLINE
PICTURE IT! ANIMATION
www.TexasReadingStreet.com

School

TEKS

K.3.B Use letter-sound relationships to decode regular words in text and independent of content.
K.3.C.1 Recognize that new words are created when letters are changed.

Envision It! Sounds to Know

Oo

otter

READING STREET ONLINE
ALPHABET CARDS
www.TexasReadingStreet.com

Phonics

Short *o*

Words I Can Blend

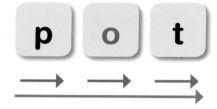

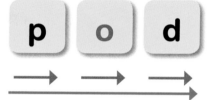

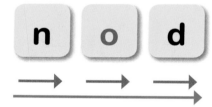

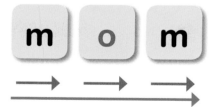

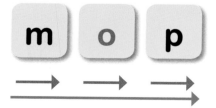

Words I Can Read

they

you

of

Sentences I Can Read

1. They like you.
2. They can see Mom.
3. Sit on top of Mom.

117

TEKS
K.3.A.1 Identify the common sounds that letters represent. **K.3.B.1** Use knowledge of letter-sound relationships to decode regular words in text. **K.3.D** Identify and read at least 25 high-frequency words from a commonly used list.

Phonics

I Can Read!

Decodable Reader

- Short *Oo*
  Rod
  top
  Don
  not
  on
  cot
  Dot

- High-Frequency Words
  the
  you
  is
  of
  they

▲ Read the story.

READING STREET ONLINE
DECODABLE eBOOKS
www.TexasReadingStreet.com

Tip the Top

Written by Page Kuhl
Illustrated by David Muntz

Decodable Reader 18

Rod can pat it.
Rod can tip the top.

Don can pat it.
Don did tip it.

You did not tip the top.

It is on top of the cot.

Dot did not tip it.

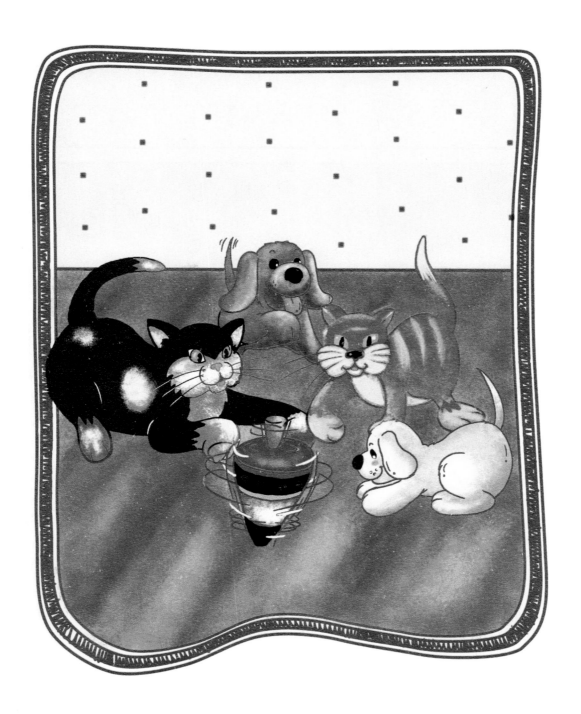

They can pat the top.
They can tip it.

It can not tip!

TEKS

K.6.B Discuss the big idea (theme) of a well-known folk tale or fable and connect it to personal experience. K.8.A.1 Retell a main event from a story read aloud.

Envision It! | Retell

Trade Book

The Lion and the Mouse

1

2

3

4

5

6

READING STREET ONLINE
RETELL
www.TexasReadingStreet.com

Think, Talk, and Write

1. How does the mouse help the lion? **Text to World**

2. What lesson did you learn from this story?

Main Idea

3. Look back and write.

TEKS

K.5.C Identify and sort pictures of objects into conceptual categories. **K.16.B.1** Speak in complete sentences to communicate. **K.23.A.1** Follow agreed-upon rules for discussion, including taking turns.

Let's Learn It!

Vocabulary

- ● Talk about the pictures.
- ■ Look around. Name things that are hard. Name things that are soft.
- ▲ Name things that are smooth.
- ★ Name things that are rough.

Listening and Speaking

- ● Ask a question about a picture.
- ■ Answer a question with a complete sentence.

Vocabulary

Words for Textures

hard

soft

rough

smooth

Ask and Answer Questions

Be a good listener!

TEKS

K.10.A Identify the topic and details in expository text heard or read, referring to the words and illustrations. **K.10.B.1** Retell important facts in text heard or read. **K.10.D** Use titles and illustrations to make predictions about text.

Lions

Let's Practice It!

1

Expository Text

● Look at the title and the pictures. What will the selection be about?

■ Listen to the selection.

▲ How do lions get their food?

★ What do lions have that helps them hunt?

♥ Why do people read selections like this one?

130

Words for Things That Go

airplane

bike

truck

car

bus

van

boat

train

Words for Colors

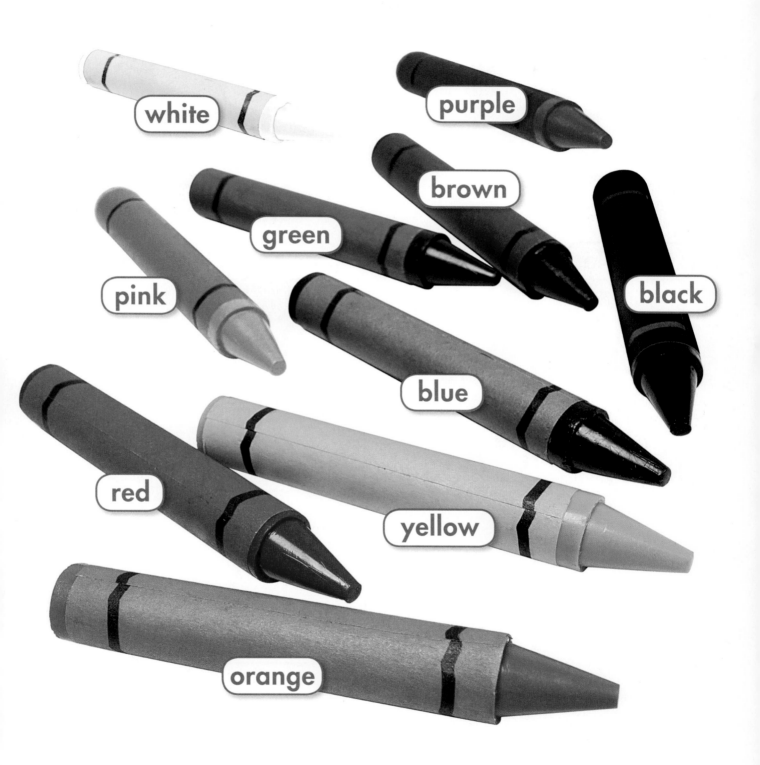

white

purple

brown

green

pink

black

blue

red

yellow

orange

Words for Shapes

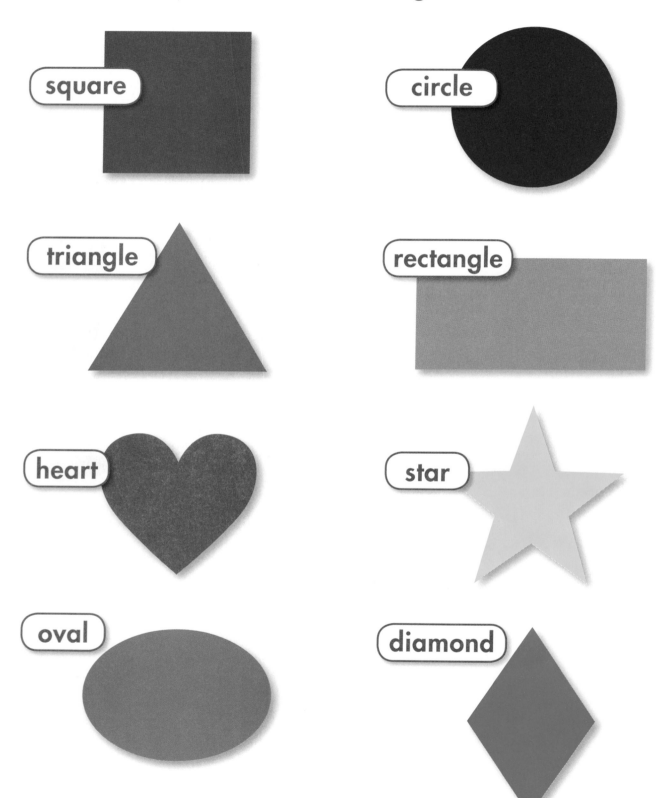

square

circle

triangle

rectangle

heart

star

oval

diamond

Words for Places

school

home

park

train station

police station

fire station

post office

library

Words for Animals

lion

mouse

puppy

dog

cat

kitten

duck

turtle

chick

hen

rooster

bird

butterfly

fish

whale

caterpillar

bear

panda

beaver

calf

cow

Words for Actions

skip

walk

run

fly

swim

ride

jump

hop

Position Words

up

down

in

out

on

around

over

under

My Classroom

bookcase

easel

books

desk

markers

crayons

pencil

teacher

toys

paper

chair

blocks

table

rug

Words for Feelings

happy

frightened

worried

excited

angry

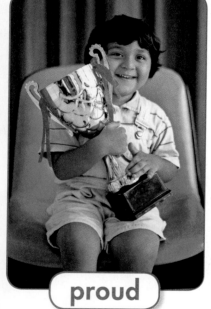

proud

sad

surprised

My Family

mom
mother

dad
father

sister

grandmother

grandfather

brother

Illustrations

Cover: Rob Hefferan

12 Mary Sullivan

28, 68, 88, 108–109 Mick Reid

30 Ken Wilson Max

32 Kellie Lewis

39–45 Natalia Vasquez

50–51 Daniel Griffo

52 Miki Sakamoto

59–65, 119–125 Maria Mola

72 Stacy Curtis

79–85 Dani Jones

90–91 Aaron Zenz

92 Suwin Chan

99–105 Wednesday Kirwan

110–111 Linda Bronson

112 Akemi Gutierrez.

Photographs

Every effort has been made to secure permission and provide appropriate credit for photographic material. The publisher deeply regrets any omission and pledges to correct errors called to its attention in subsequent editions.

Unless otherwise acknowledged, all photographs are the property of Pearson Education, Inc.

Photo locators denoted as follows: Top (T), Center (C), Bottom (B), Left (L), Right (R), Background (Bkgd)

10 (B) ©Steve Bloom Images/Jupiter Images

48 ©Chuck Franklin/Alamy Images, ©Hal Beral/Corbis, ©Mika/zefa/Corbis, Jupiter Images

49 ©Bill Frymire/Masterfile Corporation, ©Chuck Franklin/Alamy Images, ©Michael Newman/PhotoEdit, Inc.

69 ©Buzz Pictures/Alamy, ©D. Hurst/Alamy, ©DK Images, Frank Greenaway/©DK Images, Peter Chadwick/©DK Images, Tim Ridley/©DK Images

87 (B) ©Arthur Morris/Corbis, (C) ©Lynda Richardson/Corbis

89 ©Phil Savoie/Nature Picture Library, ©Philippe Clement/Nature Picture Library

128 ©Visuals Unlimited/Corbis, Corbis, Mike Dunning/©DK Images

130 (B) ©Roderick Edwards/Animals Animals/Earth Scenes

131 (T) ©ABPL/Clem Haagner/Animals Animals/Earth Scenes, (B) ©Michael Fogden/Animals Animals/Earth Scenes, (C) ©Peter Weimann/Animals Animals/Earth Scenes.